HISTORY OF
ROCKLAND COUNTY

NEW YORK,

—— WITH ——

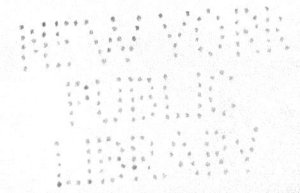

BIOGRAPHICAL SKETCHES OF ITS PROMINENT MEN.

—— EDITED BY ——

REV. DAVID COLE, D. D.

NEW YORK:
J. B. BEERS & CO.,
36 VESEY STREET.

1884.

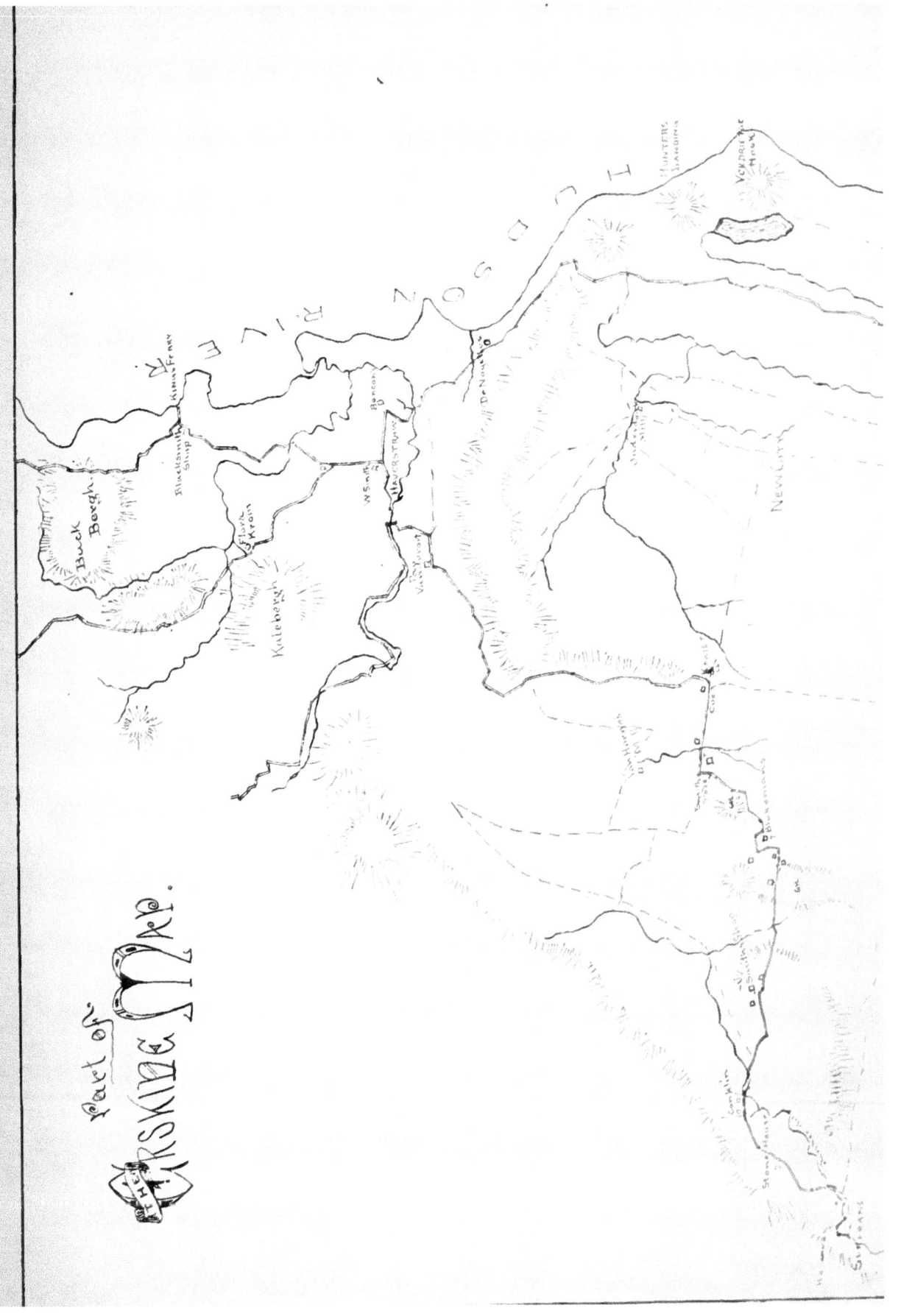

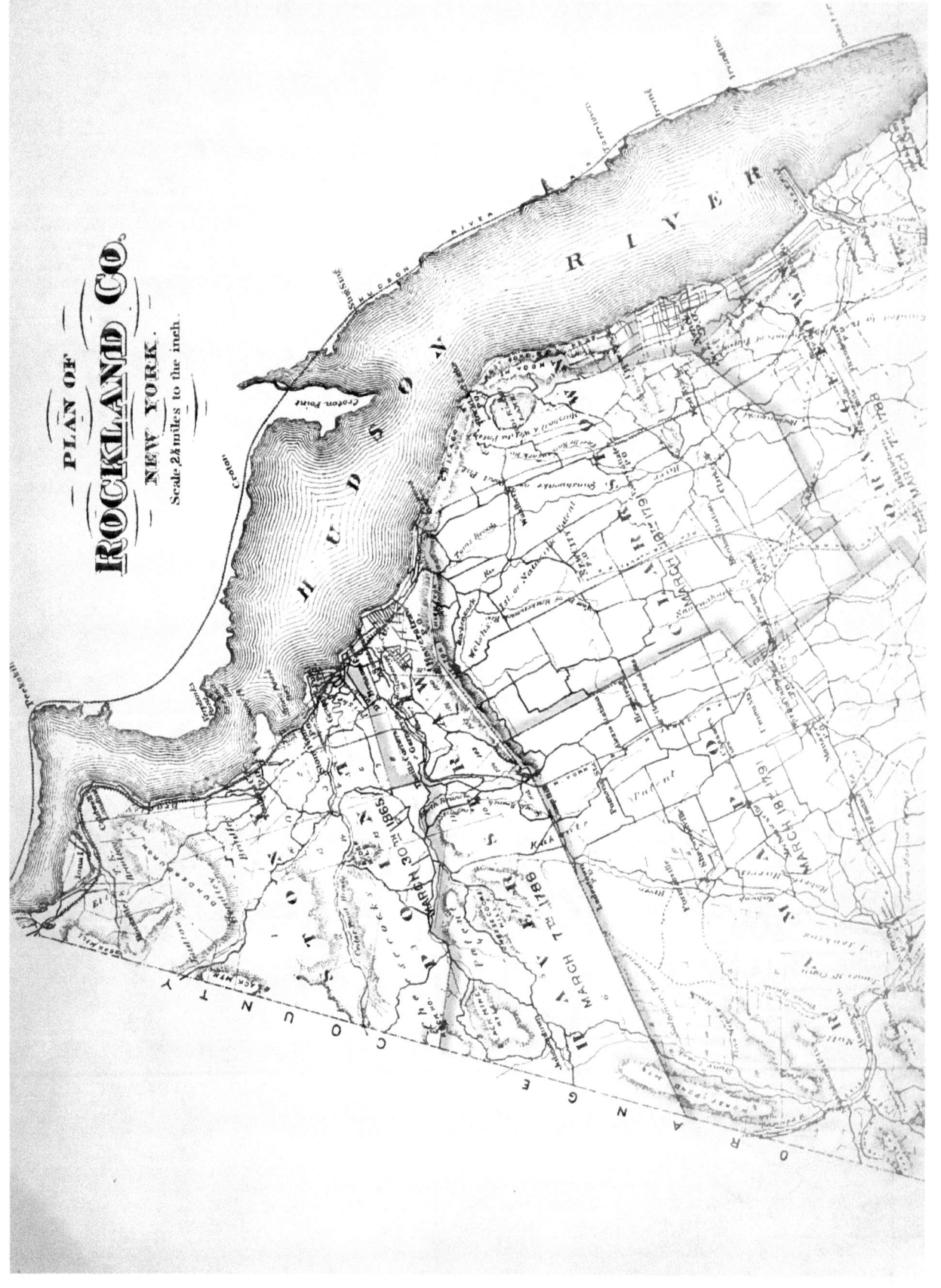

Eleazar Lord

ROSE HERMITAGE.

The Residence of GEORGE D. MACDOUGALL.

Located on the Haverstraw Road two miles from Nyack; commands a fine view of the western part of the county, including the valley of the Hackensack and the Ramapo Mountains.

Christian Dietzsch

JOHN PIERPONT'S

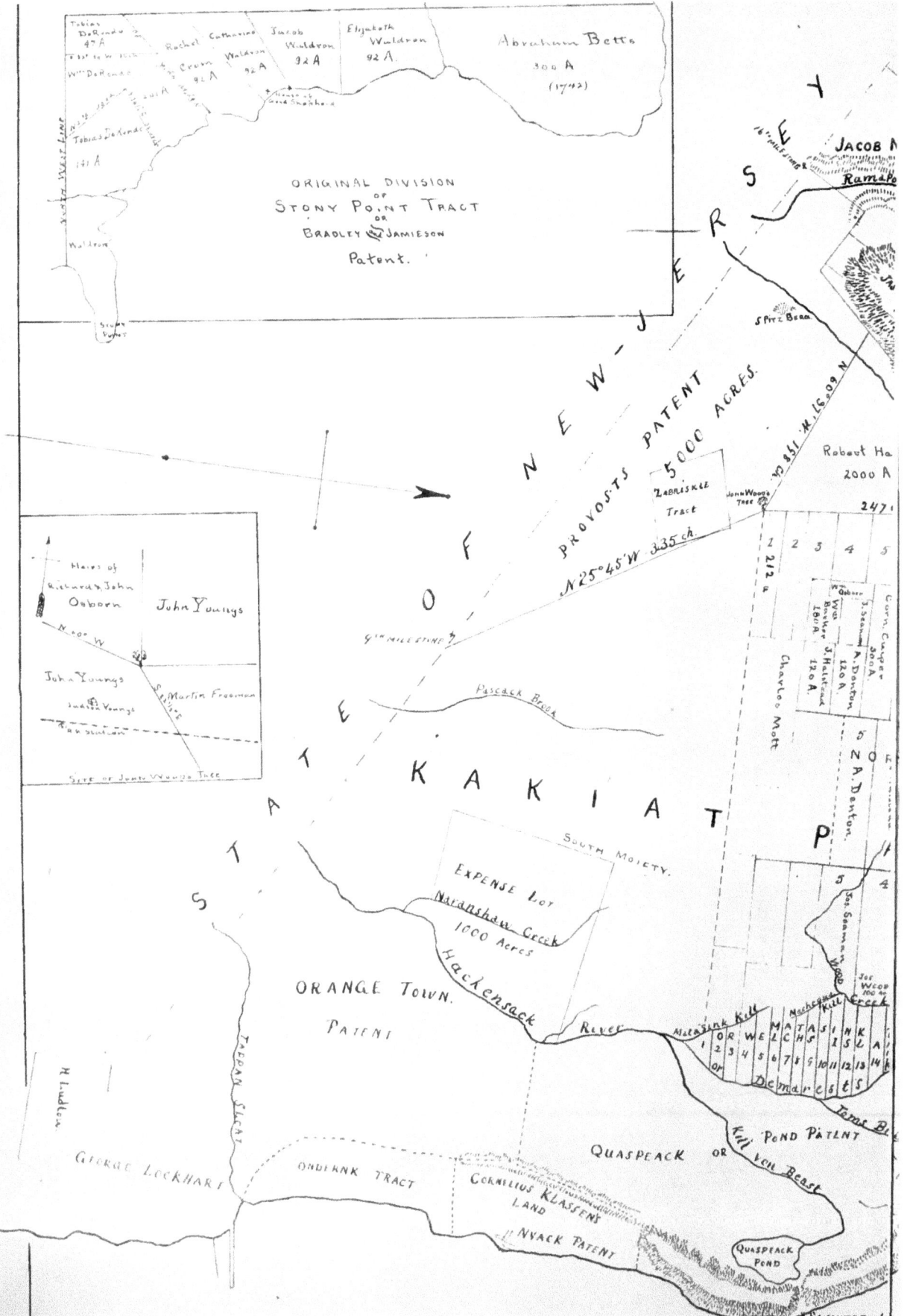

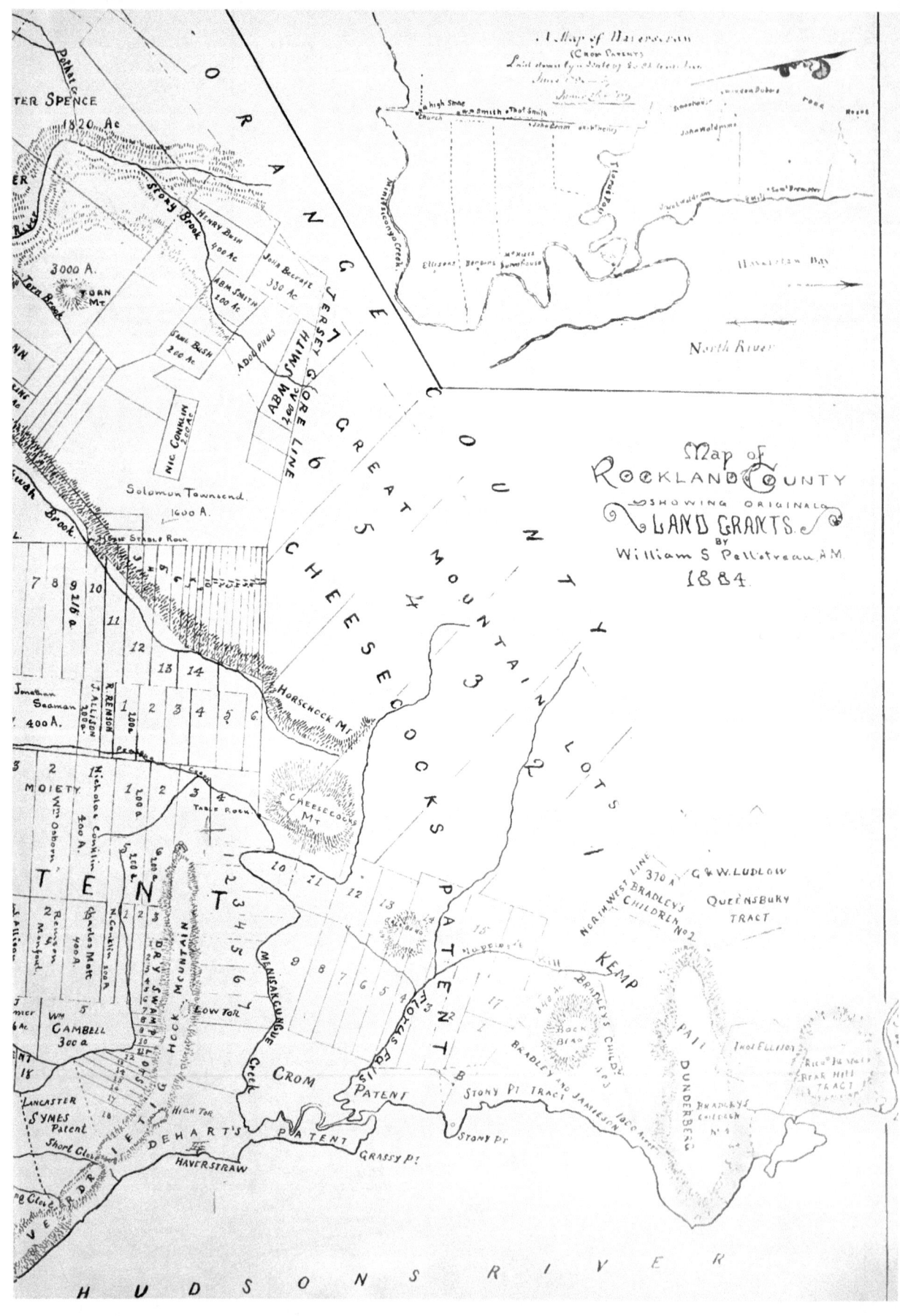

Residence of JAMES E. WEST.

WEST HAVERSTRAW, ROCKLAND COUNTY, N.Y.

HOMESTEAD OF JOSEPH B. ALLISON.
BUILT 1760.

BENJAMIN ALLISON. HOUSE.
Built 1754.

RELICS OF OLD HAVERSTRAW

JAMES G. SCOTT.

RESIDENCE OF THE JOHN PECK,
PEKIN TOMPKINS CO. N.Y.

Amasa S. Freeman

Residence of JAMES GARNER WEST,
ROCKLAND COUNTY, N.Y.

JAMES WOOD.

BRICK YARDS OF

HAV

JOHN DERBYSHIRE.
TRAW.

Phineas Hedges

Very Respectfully
John Disbrow

BUILT 1836.

REFORMED DUTCH CHURCH.

PIERMONT, N. Y.

Isaac D. Cole.

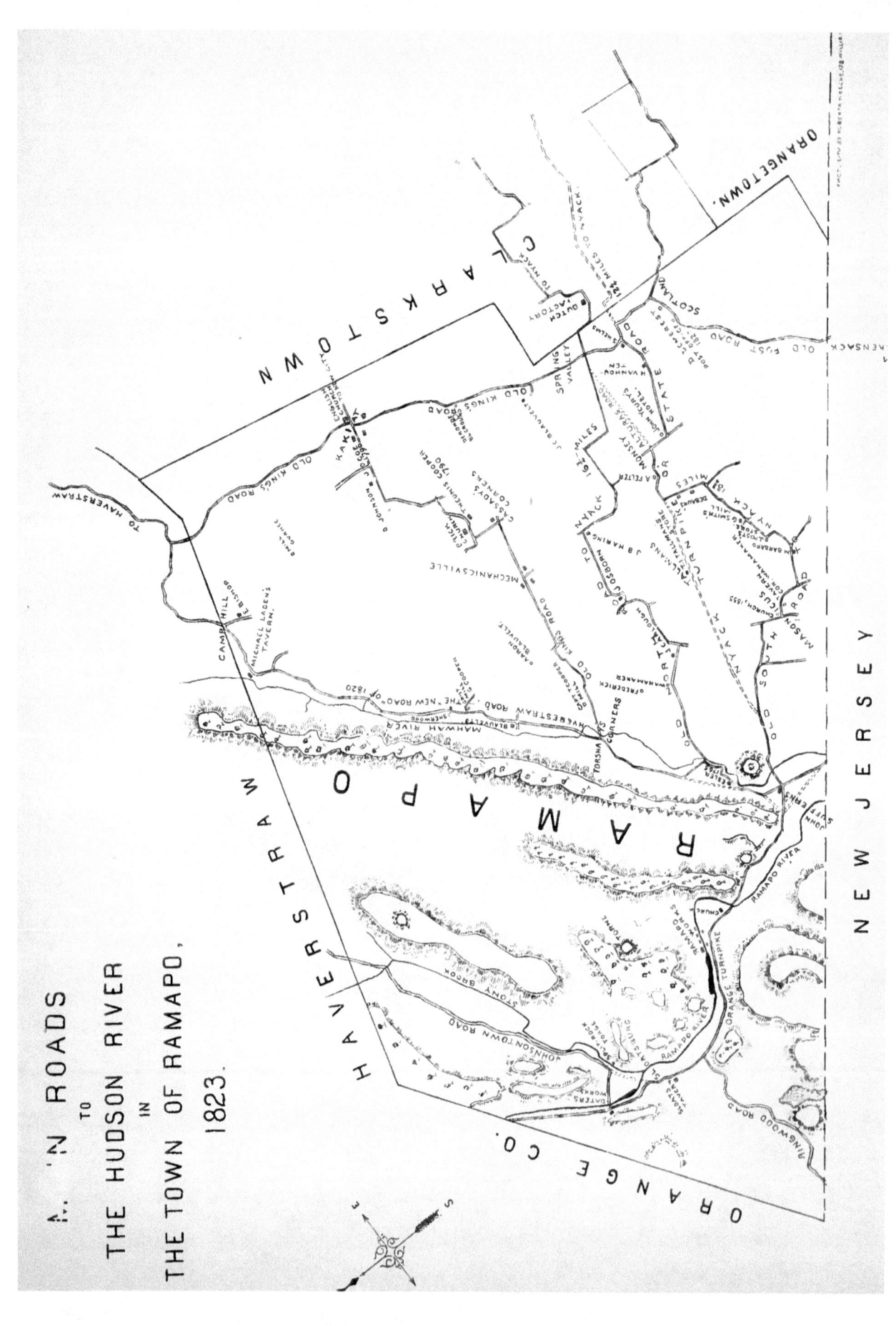

REFERENCES.

1. Nail Works, and Rolling Mill.
2. Steel Furnaces.
3. Foundry.
4. Pattern Shop.
5. Wheelwright Shop.
6. Store Room and Hoe Factory.
7. Coal House.
8. Forge and Wire Works.
9. Smith Shop.
10. Cotton Mill.
11. Dye House.
12. Screw Factory and Machine Shop.
13. Store House.
14. Coal House.
15. School House.
16. Parsonage.
17. Store House.
18. Store.
19. Grist Mill.
20. Saw Mill.
21. Straw Mill.
22. Horse Stables.
23. Oxen and Mule Stables.
24. Mule Stables.
25. Mule Stables.
26. Barn and Slaughter House.
27. Barn.
28. Carriage House.
29. Pierson Family Mansion.
30. Pierson Family Mansion.
31. Old Road through "Pass" now Orange Turnpike.

The Village extended beyond the limits of this sketch, and included the church and burying grounds, and 19 dwellings not herein shown.

RAMAPO "IN YE OLDEN TIMES."

VIEW OF STABLES & FISH POND, FROM THE EAST.

VIEW OF RESIDENCE FROM THE WEST

Erastus Johnson

*Sincerely
Eudora Shaughnessy*

E. Gay, Jr.

Will Hawkins

Theodore F. Tomkins

Daniel Tompkins

www.ingramcontent.com/pod-product-compliance
Lightning Source LLC
LaVergne TN
LVHW061217060426
835507LV00016B/1975